CountryLiving

Get Organized, Keep Everything

© 2021 by Hearst Magazines, Inc.

Book design by Izzy Lamb

Contributing Editor: Rhonda Reinhart

Photography credits on page 207

Library of Congress Cataloging-in-Publication Data is on file with the publisher.

ISBN 978-1-950099-95-5

Printed in China

4 6 8 10 9 7 5 3   hardback

HEARST

CountryLiving

Get Organized, Keep Everything

From the Editors of *Country Living*

———————◇———————

We admire the minimalists among us. We really do. We just don't understand how they do it. Here at *Country Living*, we couldn't bear the thought of parting with the bulk of our precious stuff. But here's the deal: Sometimes the stuff that sparks so much joy within us can also overwhelm us. Our collections can feel more like clutter, our closets can breed chaos, and our medley of mementos can start to feel more like something we wish we could forget. As fellow collectors, junkers, and treasure seekers, we know you know what we mean! So for the sake of our own sanity—and yours, too—we've devised a simple three-step system to bring calm to our cabinets, serenity to our shelves, and decorum to our drawers. With this organizing method, you won't have to overhaul your entire home; you'll just have to rethink what goes where. And the best part is that you won't have to throw away a single thing. Hallelujah!

In the following pages, we'll show you how to Make Your Mess Intentional (page 9), Treat Storage Like a Collection (page 81), and Organize Like an Expert (page 155). Do you have beloved pieces that you haven't seen in ages because they're crammed in the back of an overstuffed cupboard? Sometimes the solution is as simple as bringing them out of the darkness and turning them into a display instead. Are you uninspired by typical organizing tools like ho-hum plastic bins and store-bought canisters? Consider alternative containers—ones that reflect your personality and can become collections themselves. Don't know where to begin? Have no fear. We have created the ultimate list of tips and tools to get you started on the path to making every room in your house a showplace for all your prized finds—even the ones that you haven't discovered yet!

Contents

Step One   Make Your Mess Intentional 9

INTRODUCTION 11

ENTRYWAYS 12

LIVING ROOMS 20

KITCHENS & DINING ROOMS 32

PANTRIES & CLOSETS 42

BEDROOMS 48

BATHROOMS 54

KIDS SPACES 60

OUTDOORS 66

OFFICES 72

Step Two   Treat Storage Like a Collection 81

INTRODUCTION 83

ENTRYWAYS 84

LIVING ROOMS 90

KITCHENS & DINING ROOMS 100

PANTRIES & CLOSETS 112

BEDROOMS 118

BATHROOMS 126

KIDS SPACES 132

OUTDOORS 138

OFFICES 146

Step Three   Organize Like an Expert 155

INTRODUCTION 157

THE FAB 15 158

Make Your Mess Intentional

Introduction

So, what do we mean by Make Your Mess Intentional? We're talking about having a method to the madness. Our goal is not an immaculate home, a place so pristine that it's devoid of personality. While some organizing pros might disagree, we are more interested in realism than perfectionism. We want you to stop cramming your multitude of stuff into closets and drawers and cabinets—all in an effort to live up to someone else's ideal. That just creates mayhem in your storage spaces and keeps you from enjoying the treasures you've spent a lifetime acquiring. Instead—and this is where the intentional part comes in—we want you to celebrate your collections. Bring them out of the closets, drawers, and cabinets, and figure out a way to shine a spotlight on them—while, at the same time, free up those storage spaces for the things that actually need to be stored. These pages are chock-full of inspirational spaces that do just that. From flea-market finds transformed into funky gallery walls to beautiful bookshelves that turn everyday items into works of art, we have a feeling you're going to want to copycat almost everything you see. We sure do! Here's what to keep in mind as you tackle the first step in your organizing adventure.

ABUNDANCE ISN'T A BAD WORD!

As you're probably all too aware, the first order of business for most home organizing methods is to purge and part with as many items as possible. Not here! If there's one thing for certain, it's that this book will never ask you to toss something. (Yes, even if it's dusty, rusty, or beyond repair.) Why? We understand that there are some of us who derive happiness from surroundings full of trinkets and keepsakes we've acquired over the years. Each holds a memory that infuses a home with soul and substance.

CURATE THE CLUTTER.

While we're firm believers in the more-the-merrier aesthetic, we also know that no one wants to live in a mess. There's a clarity and calm that comes from an organized home. (After all, how are you supposed to enjoy and appreciate all that stuff if you don't know where it is?) This is where curation comes in. Whether built around item type, color, or function, thoughtful displays and arrangements bring eye-pleasing order to the items we love.

LOVE IT? SHOW IT!

While we won't ask you to throw anything away, we do request you play favorites now and then. With only so much surface area in any given home, choices must be made about what to display and what to store. Take stock of your "junk" and decide what items you're most eager to showcase. It can be things from single collections or a hodgepodge of treasures. There's no right or wrong answer here. The only rule is to go with your gut! And remember, a display doesn't have to be forever. Arrange things in a way that you can add or mix in new pieces in the years to come.

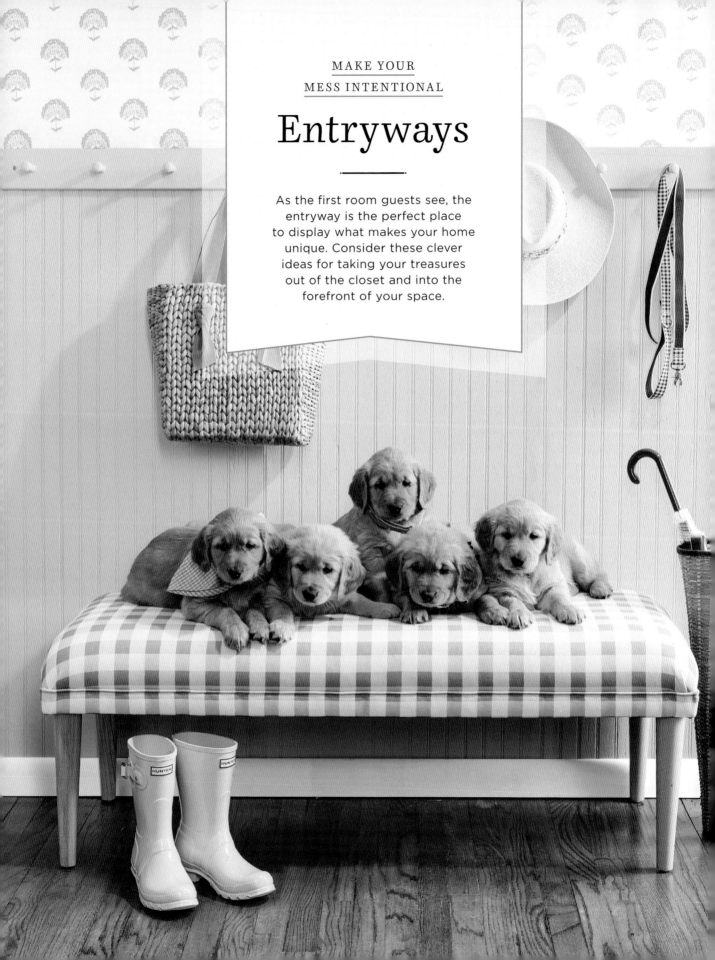

Entryways

As the first room guests see, the entryway is the perfect place to display what makes your home unique. Consider these clever ideas for taking your treasures out of the closet and into the forefront of your space.

Practical Magic!

Old washboards are magnetic, making them a country-approved alternative to a new-from-the-store memo board.

-x-x-x-x-x-x-

With the Grain

Yes, you can have it all! This small entryway is equal parts drop zone, message center, dog spot, and display area. Handsome wood-tone elements—from the antique bench to the rough-hewn shelves—bring visual unity to the multipurpose space.

In Store

A homeowner with a penchant for weathered furniture took matters into her own hands to carve out storage just inside the front door; the old general-store counter lost one row of drawers to fit the alcove's dimensions. Now each family member has a personal drawer, and the countertop serves as a bona fide display place for other chippy finds.

-x-x-x-x-x-x-

In the Bag

So long, linen closet! Vintage grain sacks get taken out of the shadows and put front and center when every family member has one to corral come-and-go belongings. Many antique sacks boast hand-stitched initials, or you can add your own with a simple cross-stitch pattern. This setup also works well in the laundry room.

Dog.

Dog Days

Live for a visit to the architectural salvage yard? Bring those finds inside! Here, a past-its-prime stock tank was transformed into a bench and dog bed, adding a splash of industrial style to this entryway. To make a hideaway for your pooch, drill holes to outline an entrance, and use a Dremel to cut an opening. Smooth the edges, and add rope trim. Make the bench top with a slab of reclaimed wood.

ROOM FOR IT ALL

This sunny entryway is stuffed to the gills with fresh ideas and hidden storage.

Vintage Fishing Creels

Just the right size for daily essentials, these carriers also add pretty woven texture.

Painted Bench

A tired wood bench was flipped sunny-side up with a coat of yellow spray paint. It makes an ideal spot for putting on shoes or stashing backpacks and totes. (The fetching look is also dog approved.)

Old Craft Letters

Unused chipboard letters were wrapped with yarn for can't-miss initials, identifying whose basket it is.

Wicker Hamper

This woven piece is an affordable, vintage alternative to a new umbrella stand. Plus, it's wide enough to hold a storage bin inside for kids to cast off socks or gloves.

-x-x-x-x-x-x-

Sew Easy

This simple Texas
entryway stitched together
hardworking storage with
upcycled industrial thread
spools. The factory relics
were mounted perpendicular
to the wall (on a faux-
weathered frame and board)
and set at varying heights for
quirky asymmetry. The nubby
collectibles are the ideal
size and shape for corralling
bags, hats, and more.

-x-x-x-x-x-x-

Giddy Up

Look closely. Tucked among the old window frames and equestrian bits is a generously sized seagrass tote bag, just right for hiding shoes. The ruffled wingback adds to the efficiency, offering a place to kick off said kicks just inside the door.

Living Rooms

Your home's designated den for relaxing, chatting, and chilling out is an ideal spot for adding some conversation pieces. Whether hung on the wall or curated on the coffee table, your favorite finds are sure to inspire a good time with these tips.

-x-x-x-x-x-x-

Basket Case

A basket collection can take up a lot of space. So if you're running short in the shelf department, hang your woven wonders to create a texture-rich arrangement. For maximum impact, display smaller catchalls around a larger piece to create a starburst pattern as shown here.

Practical
Magic!

Taking the display
all the way to the floor
makes the most
of limited wall space.

-x-x-x-x-x-x-

Camping Out

This gallery wall of campy thrift-store gems could have looked messy and
jumbled. But by sticking to a cohesive color thread—in this case primary shades
of red, blue, and green—the playful assortment feels perfectly placed.

Flower Power

Two heads are better than one. And, in this case, a bevy of blooms is better than a single bouquet. Grouping similar items together—like these vintage floral paintings cascading across green-painted shiplap—gives a gallery wall an artful look. Though the frame styles are different and the canvas sizes vary, the single subject matter creates a unified front.

MAD ABOUT THE HOUSE

PATTERN

W TO DECORATE

STYLE

WILD FLOWERS

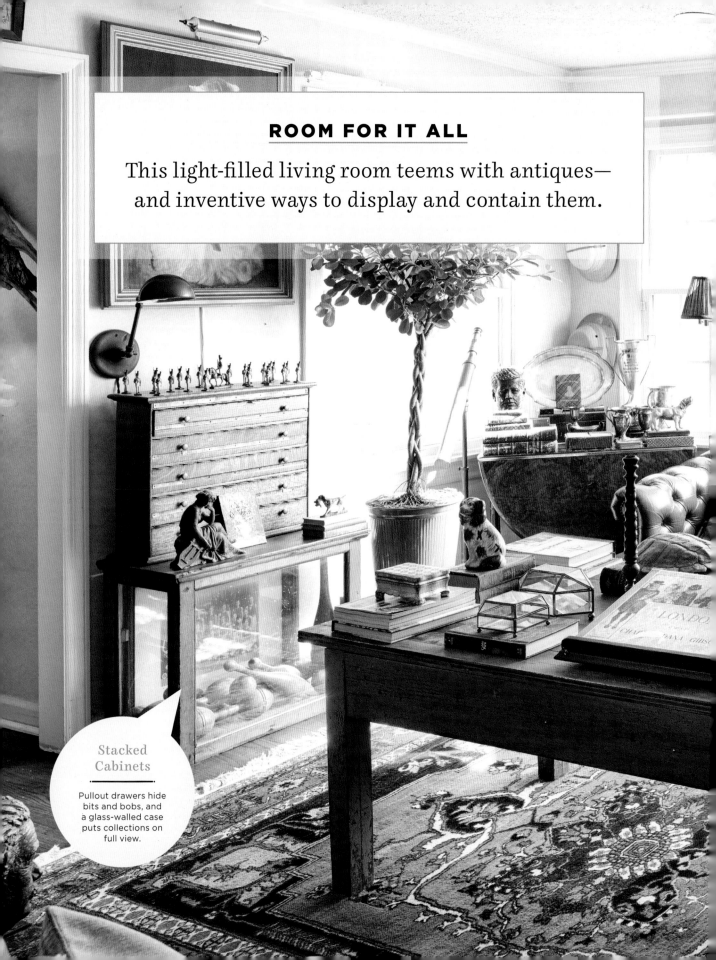

ROOM FOR IT ALL

This light-filled living room teems with antiques— and inventive ways to display and contain them.

Stacked Cabinets

Pullout drawers hide bits and bobs, and a glass-walled case puts collections on full view.

Hats on Hooks

While a hat tree is certainly a handy place to hang a chapeau, headwear as wall decor is a whole lot more fun.

Window Art

Who needs wall space? Prop a painting against a windowpane for a picture-perfect way to show off artwork.

Oversize Coffee Table

Big enough for stacks of books, fresh florals, and one-of-a-kind collectibles.

-x-x-x-x-x-x-

Stamp of Approval

Collectors of antique letters might find it tempting to tuck these pieces of postal history into a drawer for safekeeping. But as this chambray-blue living room shows, with a little bit of wall space and a few simple frames, you can free up drawer storage while paying lovely homage to the pen pals of yesteryear.

-x-x-x-x-x-x-

Hanky Panky

What's better than a collection of beautifully delicate vintage handkerchiefs? A dainty hanky collection turned patchwork curtain panel. Not only do these pretty pieces of colorfully patterned cloth add a whimsical touch to the space, but also their light-filtering sheerness softens the sunshine flowing into the room.

Practical Magic!

Prop petite paintings or framed photographs against each other and place smaller objects in front to give shelves a lovely layered look.

-x-x-x-x-x-x-

Head-Turning Hodgepodge

The Long Island antiques dealer who devised this delightful scene turned everyday items like hats, a sewing machine, and folded tablecloths into works of art by mixing them with vintage paintings, brass collectibles, and other cherished treasures.

SPIRIT LOCKER

MANOHAR

Practical Magic!

Installing a peg rail allows unwieldy items to be included in the mix.

-x-x-x-x-x-x-x-

Ships Ahoy

Grouping items by motif is a fun way to make mismatched flea-market finds look like they belonged together all along. In this sea-themed sitting area, nautical knickknacks and artwork unite to create a colorful patchwork.

-x-x-x-x-x-x-

Clock In

Instead of scattering a collection around the house, display all the pieces in one place for maximum impact. Here, a collage of clocks makes eye-popping wall art, and a stack of vintage suitcases offers extra storage.

-x-x-x-x-x-x-

Frame by Frame

Vintage silhouettes amp up the traditional vibe in a wallpapered living room. The framed portraits exhibit an array of shapes, sizes, and styles, adding visual interest to the display. For a gallery wall like this, choosing mats in the same color creates a more connected look.

Practical Magic!

Don't be afraid to use every inch of wall space! You'll add drama and ensure there are no leftover portraits that need to be tucked away in boxes or closets.

-x-x-x-x-x-x-

Get Crafty

This craft-lover in Texas turned her art supplies into artwork. Spools of sequins, pastel-dripped paint cans, and jars of glitter add a sparkly contrast to the chippy, peely, open-door hutch that houses them. And, even better, the vintage display case keeps things all in one place for easy retrieval when inspiration strikes.

Pin Pals

A homeowner bowled over by vintage wooden bowling pins took an all-or-nothing approach when it came to showcasing her impressive collection. Keeping the well-worn pieces together—in an equally weathered antique hutch—contains the chaos and proves once and for all that you can't have too much of a good thing.

Kitchens & Dining Rooms

Give the heart of your home even more love by keeping sentimental items, like your grandmother's serving dish or the flatware you found on your first flea-market trip, in full view. The strategies here will help ensure everything always looks neat, never overwhelming.

-x-x-x-x-x-x-

Open Concept

From top to bottom, this cute, sunlit kitchen lets it all hang out. With open upper shelves for everyday dishes and glasses and undermounted wire baskets for fresh produce, the space puts all of its contents on full view. Even the countertop canisters are crystal clear. Think you might have trouble keeping calm and carrying on in a kitchen with everything in plain sight? There's a way to tame the rooms-gone-wild effect you fear. Stick to just a handful of materials, and remember the rule of three: No more than three colors in a space. Here, it's black, brown, and white, but you can choose whatever trio you like!

ROOM FOR IT ALL

This baby-blue space takes kitchen storage to new heights.

Hanging Storage

A humble nail from the hardware store serves as an easy way to keep aprons accessible and on full display.

Produce Basket

A wire basket mounted under the island is a convenient container for produce, cookbooks, or anything else a recipe requires.

Cook's
Illustrated
Cookbook

Floor-to-Ceiling
Built-ins

Dual built-ins washed
in a calming blue hue
house kitchen goods
galore—and look
pretty doing it.

Mobile
Storage

Outfitted with wheels
and a handle, this
wicker basket can
easily go wherever
it's needed.

-x-x-x-x-x-x-

Going Green

When you own a collection
of great-looking kitchen
goods like these pretty
copper pieces, you should
show them off! They can
act as decor, and you can
free up cabinet space in
the process. Here, a thin
metal rod attached to a
green tile backsplash holds
small pots and measuring
cups. The movable S-hooks
allow the composition to be
rearranged with ease.

Feeling Blue

Tidy doesn't have to mean sterile.
For proof, look no further than this cheery
farmhouse-style kitchen. The well-organized
open shelves and petite peg rail offer
excellent ways to keep the space clutter free.
But the butcher-block countertop, skirted
cabinet, and blue-and-white wall make it feel
warm and inviting.

Practical Magic!

Hang rolls of paper towels
on the wall to keep
them dry and handy. Only
requirements: a small nail
and a little bit of twine.

-x-x-x-x-x-x-

Hang On

As this light and bright kitchen proves,
French rods aren't just for drapes anymore.
Here, a handy rod installed next to the stove
holds a collection of copper pots and pans,
suspended by simple leather loops with
hooks. The well-organized room's other
out-of-the-way storage solutions include a
magnetic wall-mounted knife rack and open
shelves for books and bowls.

-x-x-x-x-x-x-

Full Circle

Keeping dishware in a china closet is a perfectly acceptable way to store your tabletop goods. But why not get creative? Hanging multisize plates in a wreath formation makes for an eye-catching display, especially when they're blue and white beauties like the ones in this darling dining-room nook.

Apron Strings

-x-x-x-x-x-x-

Recipe cards and wooden spoons get a happy new home with this retro-style kitchen arrangement. Besides being downright adorable, the multihued aprons hang from an accordion peg rack and act as handy storage pockets for go-to cooking accessories. Plus, you'll never ruin another outfit when you have convenient cover-ups at the ready.

-x-x-x-x-x-x-

Let That Pony Run

No horsing around. This equine-themed dining area is chockablock with bright ideas, from vintage trophies as flower vases to horsey artwork on a gallery wall. But the hands-down most creative element is the light fixture adorned with equestrian ribbons. The whimsical display wins by a nose for its added bonus of freeing up closet space.

Nothing Bundt the Best

Are your overstuffed kitchen cabinets bursting at the seams with all your must-have baking supplies? Here's a sweet idea: Pick a baker's dozen of your favorite Bundt pans and turn them into wall art. Bonus points if the asymmetrical display includes multiple colors, a variety of sizes, and an array of styles.

-x-x-x-x-x-x-x-

Recipe for Success

Recipe cards handed down from generation to generation are keepsakes on their own. But framing them in vintage pie tins can give them pride of place on any kitchen wall. This way, they're accessible when you need them and might even keep them free of cake-batter splashes and cooking-oil stains. Add a couple of rolling pins to the mix, and you've got a baking-themed wall display that would make your great-grandmother proud.

-x-x-x-x-x-x-

Loving Spoonfuls

Instead of jamming wooden spoons into a cluttered drawer, feature the utensils prominently over a baking station. Here, the homeowner hung various shapes and sizes from light to dark, creating an ombre art installation.

Pantries & Closets

Even that which lives behind closed
doors deserves a punch of personality.
Here's how to create a sense of order
and a sense of style.

-x-x-x-x-x-x-

Cupboard Love

This petite pantry off an English country-style kitchen is paneled perfection. The narrow shelves hold plenty of provisions but don't take up too much room in the wee space. Decanted dry goods in clear-glass jars and plastic bags make the contents easy to see. And a wall-mounted rod with S hooks is an orderly place to keep aprons.

Small Space, Big Ideas

Look out below! As the owner of this Wisconsin butler's pantry knows, when you have a tiny space, you have to make the most of it. So she hung glassware on the underside of one of the open shelves and used a rod stretched across the two brackets beneath another shelf to keep rolls of paper towels.

Well Stocked

With its white beadboard walls, good-sized window, and well-organized shelves, this light, bright pantry feels like a breath of fresh air. Dry goods decanted in clear-glass jars (neatly arranged from smallest to largest) line one whole shelf. While woven baskets hold bags of snacks and folded dish towels, a wire basket handles produce.

*Practical
Magic!*

Hang a clipboard
inside the door to keep
a running grocery list,
and you'll never run
out of the fam's gotta-
have-it snacks.

-x-x-x-x-x-x-

All in a Row

Labeled baskets and
containers ensure everything
has its place in this ultra-
organized pantry. But the
wooden crates on casters
used to hold heavier items
are the most ingenious
feature. Just roll them out
when it's time to refill and
roll them back when you're
done. You won't have to drag
the crates back and forth
across the floor, leaving nasty
scratches in the process.

Plates on Display

If you have a collection of pretty plates like these, it would be a shame to conceal their beauty by stacking them on top of each other. Incorporating plate slots onto pantry shelves allows you to store plates facing forward so they can be seen in all their wonderful glory. Use the extra cabinet space to store small appliances like a slow cooker or waffle maker.

Bedrooms

If there was ever a room to let
your style run wild in, this is it.
Your home's most personal space
is primed for displays of favorite
things. Here's how to keep it feeling
calm and collected.

-x-x-x-x-x-x-

Play Dress Up

With a few well-placed antiques, you can carve out a section of the bedroom to create
a charming little dressing area. Here, an industrial-style metal rack is the perfect place
to hang go-to gowns and blouses and accessories. And the large-scale leaning mirror
lets you check out your outfit—or outfits!—in style.

Flag on the Play

Vintage nautical flags are prized finds for their graphic designs, but they're also mementos of maritime history. So don't just stuff your flag finds in a drawer. Hang them on a wall for a shipshape display.

-x-x-x-x-x-x-

Paddle Up!

This nautical-by-nature bedroom steers the theme home with ship paintings, brass sailboats, and vintage oyster cans. But it's the painted paddles at the head of the quilt-covered bed that really make a splash. Storing the paddles behind the bed when you're dry-docked makes for a creative and colorful headboard and frees up storage space, too.

-x-x-x-x-x-x-

Boot Camp

Whether you're a city slicker or a bona fide cowgirl or cowboy, your boot collection is likely a point of pride. So instead of putting your pairs in the closet, where they take up valuable space, just for kicks, try leaving them out in the open. Pristine or well worn, they'll look mighty fine lined up along the foot of the bed.

Book Smart

-x-x-x-x-x-x-

Book lovers know that there's one big drawback to being a voracious reader: where to keep those tons of tomes! In this top-floor bedroom, the homeowner took advantage of a cathedral ceiling and a bountiful vintage-book collection to create a wall-size headboard and art installation. Turning the colorful spines toward the wall made for a neutral-hued display that causes the potentially busy grouping to feel more serene. Never a bad thing for a bedroom.

Sentimental Journey

A bedroom nightstand is the ideal spot to keep items that are close to your heart. But old letters, faded photographs, and yellowed newspaper clippings can look messy strewn about. So contain your mementos in a cloche for a sweet display of nostalgia.

Practical Magic!

Place your bedside lamp on a stack of books to add height and shed more light.

Hat Trick

You don't even have to be a collector to wind up with hordes of hats on your hands. Whether it's fishing, horseback riding, gardening, or simply going out for a stroll, different activities require different headwear. While you could cram them all in the closet, you could also take a page from this homeowner's handbook and display them on the wall. Wherever you're headed, they'll always be there when you need them.

Bathrooms

Don't forget: Like any other room in your home, your bathroom can be a canvas for art, keepsakes, and other beloved items. It's all about how you arrange them. Use these ideas to guide your displays.

-x-x-x-x-x-x-

Bathing Beauty

When storage space is lacking, like in this New Jersey bathroom, you have to resort to creative solutions. Here, the homeowners looked up for an answer to their dilemma. Using the vertical wall space behind the tub, they installed a metal rod with baskets to hold bath gels and loofahs. And, above that, a metal shelf with a trio of hooks provides a place for towels, both folded and hanging.

ROOM FOR IT ALL

From antique finds to custom designs, storage solutions shine in this light-filled Tennessee bathroom.

Antique Cabinet

Using a stand-alone cabinet to hold soaps, lotions, and other potions keeps the clutter off the vanity.

Wooden Stool

Bath time becomes extra relaxing thanks to the little antique stool just big enough for a candle and fresh-cut greenery.

Towel Display

The large-scale antique is roomy enough to house stacks of towels, and the glass-front doors make them easy to see.

Sink-Side Rack

An old saddle rack next to the sink holds washcloths and jewelry.

Custom Vanity

Ideal for hidden storage—and the chicken-wire door inserts nod to the home's farmland locale.

-x-x-x-x-x-x-

Small Wonder

The powder room in this newly built South Carolina home designed in a historical style packs a big punch in a tiny space. In addition to the vintage mirror and pedestal sink, the room gets an extra dose of old-school charm thanks to the apothecary collectibles displayed in a trio of shadowboxes.

-x-x-x-x-x-x-

Great Heights

Though this traditional-style bathroom features dual sinks and mirrors, there's only one storage cabinet. That's because the floor-to-ceiling piece works twice as hard as similar furnishings. The glass-front upper cabinets display vases and shaving brushes, and the middle shelf holds a basket of washcloths and jars of cotton swabs and cotton balls. That leaves the lower cabinets to hide the towels and other bath supplies.

Mirror, Mirror

So who's the fairest of them all? It has to be this 18th-century farmhouse bathroom in Upstate New York. The homeowners' collection of antique mirrors—positioned above the sink, beside the sink, and on top of the sink!—reflects the room's natural light in the loveliest way.

Kids Spaces

Create space for little ones' imaginations to roam wild by adding a touch of magic to even the most mundane corners. Use these ideas to spark creativity and order!

-x-x-x-x-x-x-

On a Roll

There's no denying that little-kid clothes are the cutest things ever. So take a cue from the owner of this Long Island girl's room and display those pint-size duds on a rolling rack. The daughter's diminutive dresses make dainty decor, and arranging them this way leaves room in the closet for all her other girly things.

Hall Pass

Museums do it, and galleries do, too, so why not take a tip from the pros and exhibit your kids' artwork on a rotating basis? Metal cables with clips make it easy to periodically swap out their pencil drawings and Crayola creations. It also keeps the art from gathering around the house, and you can always frame your favorites and let them stay put.

Practical Magic!

A step stool boosts little ones high enough to take on curating duties, too.

-x-x-x-x-x-x-

Child's Play

It's all fun and games in this Illinois living area, where the homeowner turned her son's collection of retro toys, books, and board games into a color-coded art installation. For a winning finish, she added a vintage bingo throw pillow to the cheery checkered settee. The whole space is kid (and corgi!) approved.

MESA VERDE
NATIONAL PARK
COLORADO

1953 GLACIER
NAT'L. PARK

YELLOWSTONE PARK

NATIVE BLACK BEAR
ONE OF THE WATER FALLS
THE LOOP OVER
GreatSmokyMts
NATIONAL PARK

NATURAL BRIDGE
P

GRAND CANYON
NAT'L PARK, ARIZ.

SHENANDOAH
NATIONAL PARK, VA.

YELLOWSTONE
PARK

SKYLINE DRIVE VA.
SHENANDOAH NATIONAL PARK

GENERAL GRANT TREE
KINGS CANYON
NAT'L PARK

LONG'S PEAK
ALTITUDE, 14,255
ROCKY MOUNTAIN
NATIONAL PARK

OLD FAITHFUL

1948

BLACK CANYON
COLORADO

1963
The Watchtower
GRAND
NATIONAL

-x-x-x-x-x-x-

Parks and Recreation

Instead of gathering dust in a drawer, a collection of souvenir national park pennants becomes a colorful installation above a chippy green chest. As more pieces are acquired, the display can grow as well, moving down beside the chest or reaching up to the ceiling.

Awash in White

Old houses come with a lot of charm. But they're often lacking in one important department: closet space. In this renovated ranch house in Tennessee, the homeowner outfitted her little girl's room with an oversize white armoire to add extra storage. The vintage piece has been in the family for many years, so it's also a way to honor previous generations.

-x-x-x-x-x-x-

Vroom, Vroom

As anyone who has crunched down on a kid's toy while cruising through the house in bare feet knows, these playthings are no fun when they leave you nursing sore soles. Here, an old mail slot moves an antique toy car collection out of the danger zone and gives it a tidy place to be displayed.

MAKE YOUR
MESS INTENTIONAL

Outdoors

Make the most of your porch,
patio, or patch of grass by
bringing more than just a lawn
chair to your outdoor spaces.
Personal touches—from shelves of
collected pots to antique crates—
can warm up your exterior all year.

-x-x-x-x-x-x-

Gardener's Delight

The weathered table in this jam-packed planting shed is a catchall for tools, twine, gloves, and more. The bottom shelf, however, is all about the pots. There, a large woven basket houses an assortment of terra-cotta containers in an array of shapes and sizes.

ROOM FOR IT ALL

There's storage goodness galore in this sunny potting shed.

Antique Shutter

Wonderfully timeworn, this shabby floor-to-ceiling shutter adds a bit of color and also serves as a place to display vintage floral prints.

Wire Baskets

Small pots are contained in baskets that slide easily beneath the potting table.

Card Catalog

Seed packets, string, and other potting essentials are stealthily stashed in this vintage find.

Two-Tier Shelf

This piece does double duty, serving as a resting spot for unused pots, as well as a place to show off framed florals.

Vintage Soda Pop Crates

These handy wooden helpers hold flowers waiting to be planted.

-x-x-x-x-x-x-

In Bloom

Old soda pop crates can be used in a variety of ways.
Here, a vintage Hires Root Beer crate holds a bevy of individual
blossoms. In addition to being the base of a beautiful display,
this wooden wonder can also offer safe storage for bud vases.

Step Outside

Now here's an organizing idea worth crowing about. The owner of this Texas sunporch found old chicken coop beds and transformed them into a display case for potted flowers and herbs. The idea would work just as well for storing pots and other outdoor accessories.

MAKE YOUR
MESS INTENTIONAL

Offices

An inspiring workspace should
remind us of exactly what
we work for. Artfully fill your
station with pieces that keep
you motivated. Who knows how
much you'll accomplish!

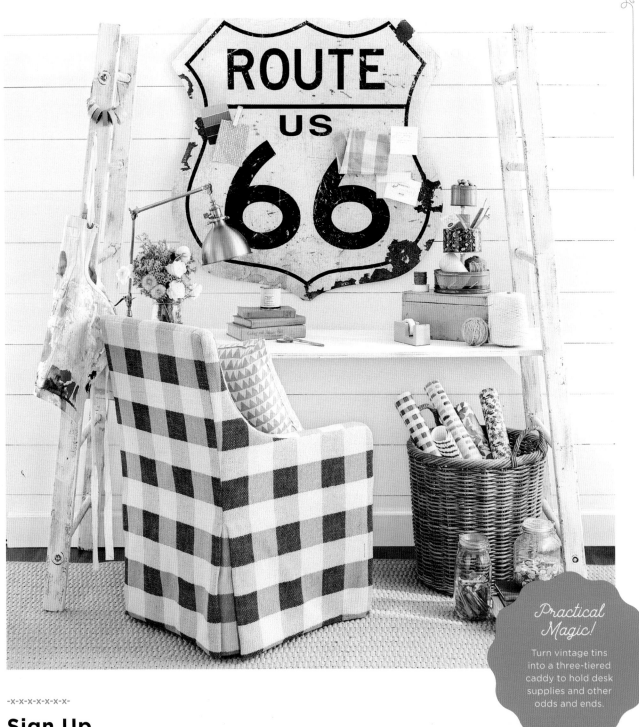

-x-x-x-x-x-x-

Sign Up

Checking off tasks never feels like a chore at this happy-go-lucky workstation—everything you need is right at the ready, thanks to a host of helpful storage ideas. Besides the rusty road sign that acts as a bulletin board, there's a tall woven basket for wrapping paper, clear jars for miscellaneous items, and repurposed ladders ideal for holding craft aprons.

Practical Magic!

Turn vintage tins into a three-tiered caddy to hold desk supplies and other odds and ends.

-x-x-x-x-x-x-

Tip Jars

Craft supplies have never looked as tidy as they do in this put-together
workspace. Easy-to-find glass jars line the shelves of a vintage hutch,
each containing a different type of item. Whether it's buttons, beads, or
string, this technique lets you store what you need for any project. And
because the jars are clear, you'll always know what's there.

Perfect Tin

You'll never have to scramble for a pencil, pen, or pair of scissors with this easily accessible setup. Colorful vintage tins hold essential supplies and brighten up wooden shelves. You can try this trick in the garage, too, filling the cans with screwdrivers, pliers, and other tools.

ROOM FOR IT ALL

Everything in this Texas crafts room is perfectly patinaed. It's also perfectly organized.

Old Display Board

Once used to display wrenches, this 1950s store sign has a new life holding strings of beads.

Hanging Hutch

The open doors on this wall-mounted hutch allow easy viewing of all its contents.

Wooden Cabinet

Two deep drawers keep unsightly items hidden away, while the timeworn top is perfect for showing off prettier pieces.

Vintage
Counter Rack

Rescued from the
junk pile, this old shop
rack is a handy way
to store paints, tape,
brushes, and more.

Tall
Table

This weathered table
is a great height for
standing work, and
a lower shelf helps
keep bulky items out
of the way.

Top Shelf

A personal study is an ideal spot to keep souvenirs, collectibles, and mementos. Here, the homeowner used a host of unlikely vessels to hold keepsakes and office supplies. A wooden crate containing old letters, a vintage trophy holding No. 2 pencils, and a ceramic pitcher with twine and scissors are just a few of the fresh ideas on this well-styled shelf.

-x-x-x-x-x-x-

Tailor Made

The designer of this pretty-in-pink sewing room came up with some unexpected ways to display and store everything a needleworker needs. From the toolbox caddy filled with thread, string, and pompom fringe to the "shelves" made from a repurposed drawer and an embroidery hoop, the common thread is that each oh-"sew"-special idea is more clever than the last.

State of Mind

-x-x-x-x-x-x-

A simple wall-mounted storage bin becomes a point of state pride when you affix an old license plate on the front of it. Here, a vintage Illinois plate pays homage to the Land of Lincoln. It's a convenient spot to stash various office supplies, and its bright red hue adds a color pop to the room.

Treat Storage Like a Collection

Introduction

Now that you've discovered clever ways to show off your most treasured pieces, you should have some extra room in your closets, drawers, and other tucked-away storage spaces to stash your not-as-pretty items, like paperwork and toiletries. This is when the true organizing begins. But, as always, we want this step to reflect your personality as much as your decorating does. Too many organizing methods take the personality out of storage, which also sucks the joy out of it. You've seen all the sterile dividers and plastic bins out there. Totally boring—we agree. When you think of your junk drawer's primary purpose not as organizing your junk but instead as a place to proudly display it every time it is opened, the pursuit becomes creative and way more fun. That's what we mean by Treat Storage Like a Collection. But this step isn't all about appearance—although we do love it when storage solutions are pretty. (We're looking at you, woven baskets and vintage hatboxes!) It's also about creating a more efficient household. When everything has a dedicated place in the home— whether it's the kitchen, laundry room, or entryway— you always know where to find it, which saves you time and stress. Before beginning this next step, consider these helpful hints.

CUPBOARDS AND DRAWERS SHOULD DELIGHT—NOT FRIGHT!

We know it's tempting to cram cabinets full, let closets burst at the seams, and overstuff drawers, but you must resist the urge. This haphazard approach won't do you any favors when it comes time to retrieve what you need. The good news is that you don't have to grab a trash bin to make room for all your belongings. With a little thoughtfulness, some quick rearranging, and a few well-placed organizing essentials, those once nightmarish storage areas can become the stuff of dreams.

THINK BEYOND PLASTIC BINS.

Standard store-bought plastic containers can certainly get the job done, but when it comes to organizing beloved collections, we say think outside the bin! Whether you need to store basics like office supplies and kitchen goods—or more sentimental items— choose an uncommon container that reflects your personality. Should it be glass jars? Vintage tins? Antique trophies? That's for you to decide. There's just one thing we know for sure: Your cherished treasures deserve the extra attention.

EVERYTHING CAN HAVE A PLACE, NO MATTER HOW MUCH YOU HAVE.

It's a tale as old as time. Once you start a collection, there's no end in sight. Even if you try to curtail your own collecting, if people know about your penchant for a particular item, you can expect gifts galore that fit that theme. But, hey, that's okay! Too much is never enough, right? So we don't want you to worry about paring down. We just want you to focus on making room. No matter the item— or, really, items—there's a creative storage solution to be found.

Entryways

As the drop spot for everyday essentials from shoes to car keys, your entryway needs to stay organized 24/7. Luckily, putting things back in their place becomes much more fun when you try these hardworking ideas.

-x-x-x-x-x-x-

Measuring Up

As veteran junkers and antique-furniture shoppers know, you should never leave home without a measuring tape. But when it comes to vintage rulers, let them stay at the house, where you can turn them into an ingenious accordion wall rack. Hang your DIY creation in the entry, and your keys and coats will always have a place to rest.

Stand and Deliver

Mudrooms can get messy fast, so you need a way to moderate the madness. Here, a three-tiered galvanized stand acts as a catchall for keys, sunnies, mints, and more. Add a petite plant to the mix, and this hardworking holder becomes a piece of decor, too. This technique works well with art supplies, kitchen goods, and bathroom necessities, too.

Rack 'Em Up!

Installed at the entry, standard wall-mounted racks are great for holding coats, umbrellas, keys, and more. But the basic store-bought variety often comes with only a few hooks. And let's be real: We have a lot of stuff. In this mudroom entrance, a repurposed bottle drying rack offers room for a multitude of items to hang simultaneously, from oversize totes to cozy sweaters.

Practical Magic!

Choose suitcases in the same color family for a cohesive look. Or try stacking them from light to dark to create an ombre effect.

-x-x-x-x-x-x-

(Suit)Case the Joint

Talk about a fantastic voyage! This elegant entrance hall travels back in time with vintage suitcases stacked jumbo to pint-size for a floor-to-ceiling storage solution that's first class all the way. Keep old family photo albums in the easier-to-access upper cases, and you can take a stroll down memory lane whenever the fancy strikes.

-x-x-x-x-x-x-

Chop, Chop

The firewood storage solution
in this sunny, whitewashed
entryway works wonders
for two main reasons. First,
keeping the rustic wood in
plain sight creates a warm and
textural display that brings the
outside in. Second, the shelf
above the woodpile provides a
chic place to showcase favorite
art and accessories.

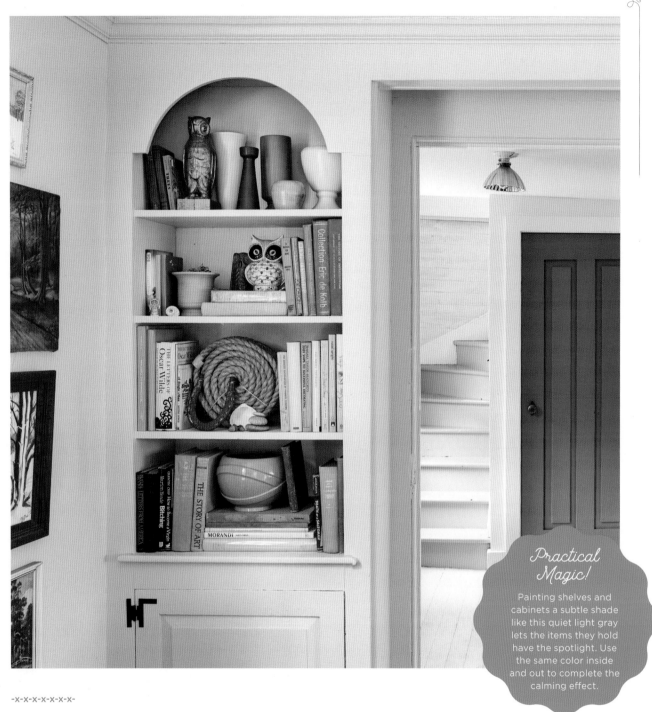

-x-x-x-x-x-x-

Shelf Life

What's so great about built-ins? Short answer: Everything! These elegant arched beauties in a 300-year-old house in Connecticut act as a single catchall case for the homeowner's assorted collections. Vintage books, one-of-a-kind objects, and a variety of vessels fill the shelves, but the pieces' similar (and subdued) palette keeps things looking cohesive.

Living Rooms

Certain elements of your living room (this month's magazines, extra blankets, remote controls) require a dedicated home to ensure quick and easy access. Here's how to beautify these essential storage areas.

-x-x-x-x-x-x-

No Heat Required

What to do with a nonworking fireplace? If it can't provide warmth, let it at least provide storage! Stack books and magazines in the unused firebox to keep reading material out of the way, then top the mantel with favorite artwork and collectibles to turn the erstwhile heat source into an instant focal point.

At A Clip

When it comes to showing art in your home, it's time to reframe the way you think. As in, who needs frames anyway? Here, simple clipboards hung by strings hold pretty pieces of paper ephemera, making it easy to change out art according to mood or season. This approach would also work well for storing and displaying family photographs.

Booking Good

Most people who use old wooden crates for storage set them on the floor, a shelf, or a tabletop. But these resourceful homeowners turned several different size crates on their ends to "build" a charming bookcase. Now their vintage book collection has an era-appropriate place to call home.

-x-x-x-x-x-x-

Double Duty

The massive antique hutch in this Texas sitting area lived its first life in an old country store. Here, the repurposed piece serves two purposes: Thanks to its open shelves and drawers aplenty, it's a display case for vintage bowls, crocks, pitchers, and more, as well as a storage place for odds and ends.

-x-x-x-x-x-x-

Quilt Trip

Handmade quilts can be works of art, so don't hide them away in a cupboard. Leave that space free for your less attractive items, and bring these colorful creations out into the light. Hanging them on the wall is a surefire way to let them shine, but draping them on an antique orchard ladder is a clever way to display several quilts at once.

-x-x-x-x-x-x-x-

And the Winner Is...

Say you have a wonderful cabinet with two-drawers. On its top you like to display your favorite collection. Now say you acquire more pieces in that collection—so many pieces, in fact, that they no longer fit on the top of the cabinet. Does that mean you should stop collecting? Not at all! Just pull out those drawers and let the overflow items live there. Here, the prized pieces are vintage trophies, but the same goes for vases, figurines, or other tall collectibles.

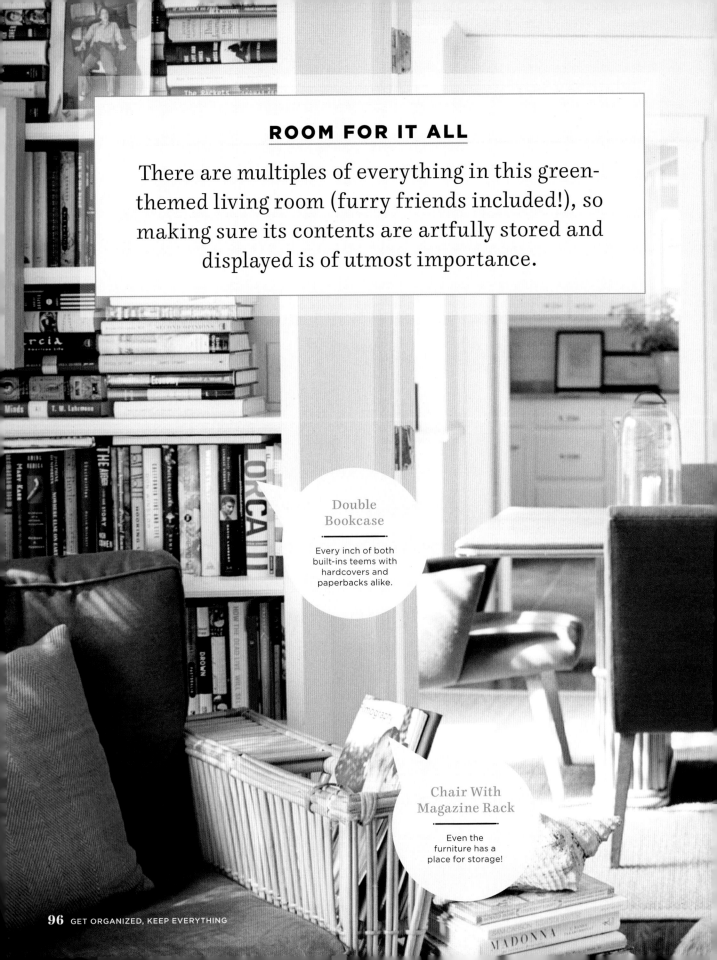

ROOM FOR IT ALL

There are multiples of everything in this green-themed living room (furry friends included!), so making sure its contents are artfully stored and displayed is of utmost importance.

Double Bookcase

Every inch of both built-ins teems with hardcovers and paperbacks alike.

Chair With Magazine Rack

Even the furniture has a place for storage!

Dining Room Cabinet

The green scheme continues in the adjacent dining area, where an antique cabinet offers even more storage, as well as a place to display an additional vase.

Round Table

A glass-topped table is home to more green vases, plus a favorite candle.

The Straight and Narrow

-x-x-x-x-x-x-x-

On the opposite end of this light-filled lounge area lies a cozy brick-surround fireplace. So when it came time to fill the room's floor-to-ceiling storage nook, the homeowner knew just what to grab: books, blankets, and firewood. The trio adds an organic touch, as well as splashes of color, to the white-walled space.

Side Hustle

The salvaged galvanized bin in this cheery living space puts the "fun" in multifunctional. Not only does it serve as a unexpected side table, but it also offers a discreet storage opportunity. Just pop the top, and you've got a handy receptacle for blankets, extra throw pillows, or whatever else you hope to hide away.

-x-x-x-x-x-x-

Game On

For smaller homes, a chest may be your best bet for storing blankets and throws. Its sturdy, flat top adds extra surface space for resting books or beverages, as it does for this homeowner.

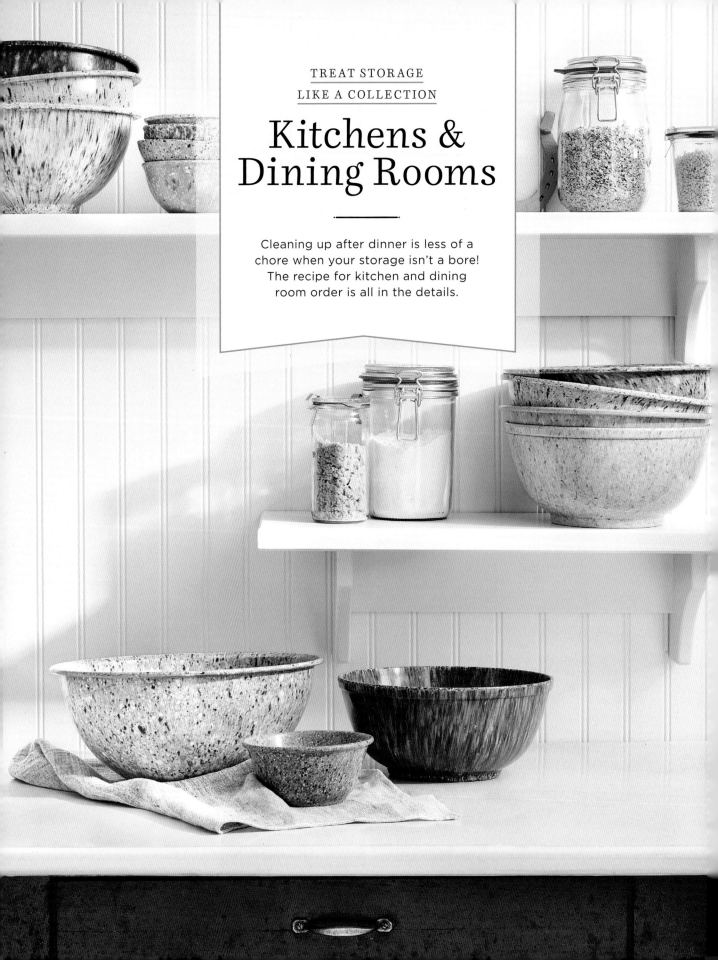

Kitchens & Dining Rooms

Cleaning up after dinner is less of a chore when your storage isn't a bore! The recipe for kitchen and dining room order is all in the details.

-x-x-x-x-x-x-

Scrub-a-Dub

This clever DIY project introduced a multifaceted storage option to a cute country kitchen. The wee washboard acts as a cabinet door, hiding spices and small utensils, and the bottom shelf holds salt-and-pepper shakers and a box of favorite recipes. Even the top of the piece is a place to stash go-to kitchen goods.

Baker's Choice

The owners of this South Carolina Low Country kitchen scored big when they found the punched-tin antique pie safe with original blue paint. But it's the hatboxes atop the piece that deserve a nod for creativity. The vintage boxes—in colors that complement the cabinet—are an unexpected choice for kitchen storage, but they work well to stash recipe cards and other necessities.

Practical Magic!

Adding a skirt beneath glass-front cabinets conceals less-than-pretty pieces.

Tight Squeeze

Space is at a premium in this narrow kitchen in a Maryland bungalow. So the homeowner opted for woven totes to stash away dish towels. The totes add natural texture to the all-white, galley-style space. When wash day rolls around, the towel-filled totes can easily be carried to the laundry room.

SEL

SALT

Pass the Salt

Hanging vintage saltcellars on a pegboard is a fun and easy way to create extra storage in the kitchen. But these diminutive and colorful containers are more than a means of organization. By grouping them together as a charming little assortment, you can create an instant art installation, too.

Sel

SALT

-x-x-x-x-x-x-

Crate Expectations

With its chic brass pendant, woven chairs, striped rug, and traditional table, this classic dining room is delightfully dignified. But there's one surprising plot twist in the space: The vintage soda pop crates used as extra seating add funky flair to the room. Even better, just lift the comfy cushion, and the crates act as extra storage for the fancy flatware and table linens that make an appearance for special occasions.

-x-x-x-x-x-x-x-

Green With Envy

A Jadeite-loving homeowner with limited shelf space concocted a
brilliant plan for storing pieces that wouldn't fit with the rest of the
collection. By installing a dowel beneath the bottom shelf and adding
a few inexpensive S-hooks to hold extra teacups, this collector made
use of empty space and created a lovely display in the process.

ROOM FOR IT ALL

This bright-idea-rich kitchen is filled to the brim with creative storage solutions.

Spice Tins

Magnetic vintage tins stick to the fridge and hold scissors, pens, and more.

Bound Books

Vintage cookbooks tied together with twine serve as nifty knife storage.

Clothespin Bag

Fresh flowers hang out in a sack suspended in the window.

Globe Stand

A roll of paper towels fits perfectly in this frame that was formerly the home of a globe of the world.

-x-x-x-x-x-x-

Take A Stand

In a cozy kitchen, every inch counts. Instead of leaving out shakers and other go-to cooking tools, free up some counter space and reimagine an extra cake stand as a shelf. A scalloped pedestal, like the one used here by a New York homeowner, adds a little whimsy to an otherwise plain display.

SANDWICHES

CLUB	25
CHICKEN	20
CUBE STEAK	20
WESTERN	15
FRIED HAM	10
HAM and EGG	15
SARDINE	10
FRIED BACON	10
" PORK CHOP	10
" EGG	10
BOILED HAM	10
HAMBURGER	10
CHEESE	10
ROAST BEEF	
" PORK	
LETTUCE	5

-x-x-x-x-x-x-

What's for Dinner?

Vintage case goods pulled from long-gone general stores are great ways to add extra storage to a space, so when you come across one of these salvaged gems, you better grab it! In this dining room, a wall-length hutch with subdivided sections allows easy organization for different types of items.

-x-x-x-x-x-x-

Mother of Reinvention

Besides using an old store counter as a hardworking island (the back side is open, offering plenty of space for canned goods and jarred foods), the owner of this Indiana kitchen repurposed feed troughs for wall storage. Here, she filled the troughs with bunches of herbs and greens, but they could also work for cookbooks and kitchen towels.

-x-x-x-x-x-x-

Knife Skills

Now here's a sharp idea: Turn an old wooden ruler into a magnetic knife rack. This DIY project will add some vintage charm to any kitchen and keep knives safely stored away. To make your own, cut the ruler into two pieces and attach on top of each other, then drill several holes in both sections, insert a magnet in each hole, and fill with wood glue.

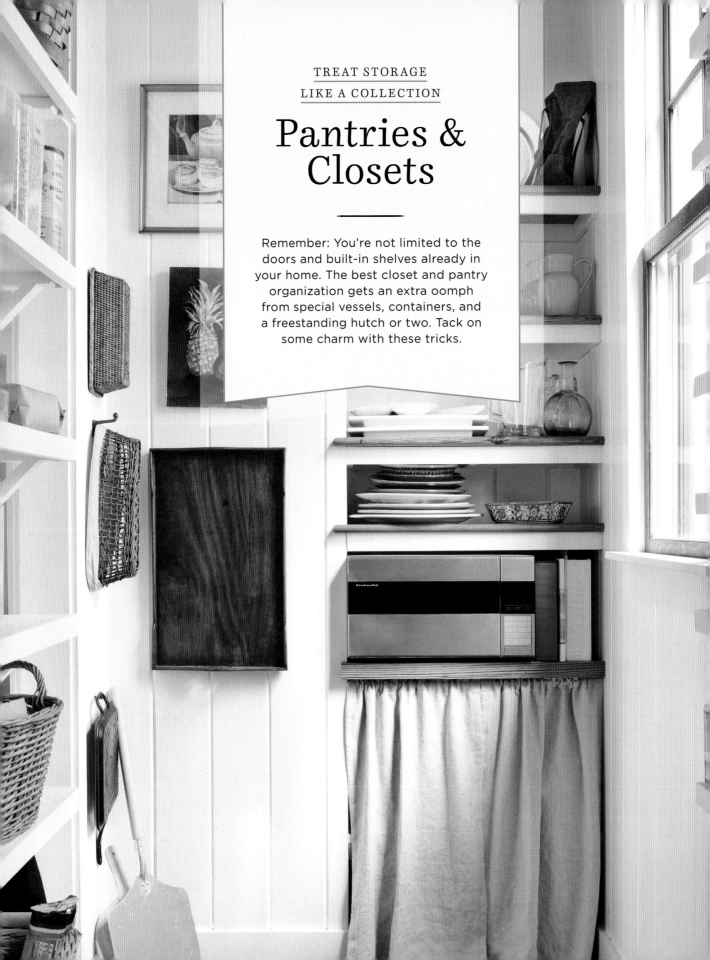

Pantries & Closets

Remember: You're not limited to the doors and built-in shelves already in your home. The best closet and pantry organization gets an extra oomph from special vessels, containers, and a freestanding hutch or two. Tack on some charm with these tricks.

-x-x-x-x-x-x-

Moo-ving Display

A Texas homeowner with a hankering for reclaimed case goods used an old general-store fridge to house her pantry staples. Come dinnertime, the glass doors make it easy to see what fixings she has available, and when it's time to go on a grocery run, she can easily tell when she's running low on spices, canned goods, and other necessities. Plus, her cute cow collection feels right at home on top of the hutch.

ROOM FOR IT ALL

This jam-packed closet turned organized utility room uses every inch of available space.

Peg Rail

Perfect for hanging brooms, dusters, and scrub brushes.

Rolling Bin

This convenient hamper on wheels tucks in neatly next to the stacked washer and dryer.

Woven Baskets

A variety of baskets keep detergent, spray bottles, and other necessities nicely in reach.

French Rod

Freshly pressed shirts and blouses hang from a rod installed on the underside of an upper shelf.

Open Shelves

Clothespins, linen sprays, and other laundry-day go-tos are easily accessible thanks to an open-concept shelving system—painted blue to match the festive floral wallpaper.

STEELE

Detergent

-x-x-x-x-x-x-x-

Open Door Policy

This freestanding kitchen hutch keeps its pantry staples neatly organized in deep metal baskets, and a galvanized tub on the bottom shelf safely stores breakable glass bottles.

-x-x-x-x-x-x-x-

Here for the Pantry

When it comes to organizing, there's more to life than plastic boxes, and this warm and welcoming kitchen knows it. Instead of run-of-the-mill bins, these pantry shelves hold baskets and vintage tins to keep contents tidy. The space also makes excellent use of mason jars, which hold pickled vegetables in addition to decanted dry goods.

What a Dish!

Antique furnishings are beautiful to look at but often aren't functional in our modern lives. As you can tell from this dishy display, that doesn't mean you can't make them work for you. Here, a wooden shelf custom built to fit inside an antique armoire holds neatly arranged dishes, glasses, linens, and more. A variety of attractive containers keep the cabinet organized: a long wicker tray for napkins, a small crock for utensils, and woven baskets for larger items. Now the heirloom piece is pretty inside and out!

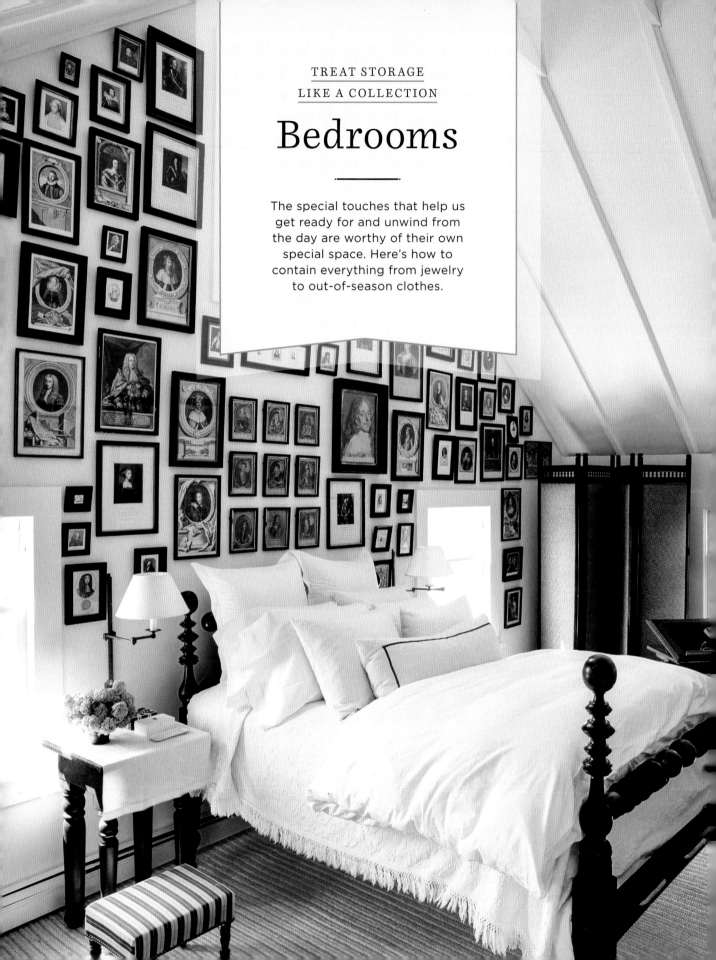

Bedrooms

The special touches that help us get ready for and unwind from the day are worthy of their own special space. Here's how to contain everything from jewelry to out-of-season clothes.

Practical Magic!

Pincushions placed in a tin or two hold brooches and stud earrings.

-x-x-x-x-x-x-

Gem Dandy

Lost rings, tangled necklaces, a single earring. Such are the plights of jewelry wearers the world over. But here's a sweet solution for errant accessories: tart tins inside a bedroom drawer to store and separate beloved jewelry pieces. Available in various sizes, the tins work for a variety of items.

-x-x-x-x-x-x-

Plum Perfect

Here, two stacked steamer trunks act as extra storage and a catchall
nightstand, holding books, a clock, jewelry, and fresh flowers. The versatile
trunks could also be used alone as a coffee table in bedrooms that have a
separate sitting area or in other informal areas.

Pretty on the Inside

It's what's on the inside that counts, right? And that goes for drawers, too. Here, patterned paper lines the drawer of a bedside table, adding a pop of color and giving the owner a treat every time it's opened. Try this trick with wrapping paper, wallpaper, old maps, or book pages.

THANK YOU

Wired Up

DIY activities are best when they're easy (meaning anyone could do them), and this quick project definitely falls into that category. With a little bit of copper wire and some old teapot lids, you can create a touching tribute to family members near and far. This idea would also work well with postcards or other paper mementos.

-x-x-x-x-x-x-x-

Trunk Show

Stacked vintage trunks add yet another layer of color in
this already hue-loving Michigan bedroom. The double
pieces do double duty as a bedside table and added
storage, where the bold-decor-loving homeowners can
stash blankets, sheets, and extra pillows.

Sleepaway Camp

Old cozy cottages are notorious for their limited storage and closet space. And the same is true for this camp-themed little boy's room. Thanks to the sticker-covered vintage footlocker, though, there's room to tuck away games and toys. Hanging rackets on the wall also frees up room in the closet.

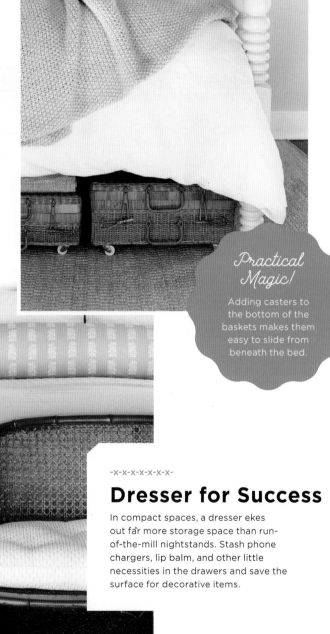

-x-x-x-x-x-x-
Roll On

Vintage picnic baskets are practically perfect for all sorts of storage. Here, two woven ones fit under the bed for stashing extra sheets and blankets. They add natural texture to the room and are way more visually interesting than typical plastic bins.

Practical Magic!

Adding casters to the bottom of the baskets makes them easy to slide from beneath the bed.

-x-x-x-x-x-x-
Dresser for Success

In compact spaces, a dresser ekes out far more storage space than run-of-the-mill nightstands. Stash phone chargers, lip balm, and other little necessities in the drawers and save the surface for decorative items.

TREAT STORAGE
LIKE A COLLECTION

Bathrooms

Given all the jobs our bathrooms
must do for us, it's rare to find
one with enough built-in storage.
Fear not: You can easily keep
everything at arm's reach when
you mix in these ideas.

-x-x-x-x-x-x-

Perfect Scents

Of course, a medicine cabinet can contain your perfume collection, but then you can't see the pretty bottles. And the top of a vanity works, too, but that can start feeling cluttered before you know it. So what's a fragrance lover to do? To experience the sweet smell of organizational success, hit the home improvement store and pick up an assortment of corbels. The architectural elements are just the right size to hold a single bottle.

-x-x-x-x-x-x-

Sweet Spot

Once used for holding liquid sugar that would eventually turn to a solid, old wooden sugar molds today are often used as decor, holding candles or tiny plants. But in this light-filled bathroom, the homeowner placed her vintage mold on the windowsill and filled it with makeup brushes and other toiletries.

-x-x-x-x-x-x-

Bring a Bench

A wooden bench serves as
the perfect perch for extra
towels and toiletries. Its
slim profile—it juts out only
a few inches from the
wall—makes it ideal for
smaller bathrooms. Think
of it as a shelf that doesn't
require hanging!

Thinking Inside the Box

-x-x-x-x-x-x-

Hats off to this ingenious scheme. Vintage hatboxes mounted on the wall hold hand towels, washcloths, and extra toilet tissue. Even better, the boxes' playfully patterned designs—stripes, solids, and polka dots, oh my!—add pops of color to the otherwise simple space.

-x-x-x-x-x-x-

Natural Touch

Sinks aren't the only place for installing some clever clutter-hiding curtains. This homeowner skirted a bathroom ledge with a classic blue and white pattern, adding a mood-boosting pop of color and some stealthy storage space for essentials. The curtain rings glide smoothly over the rod so grabbing what you need is a cinch.

TREAT STORAGE
LIKE A COLLECTION

Kids Spaces

Creative storage transforms cleanup
into playtime. These delightful
solutions may just inspire little ones
to lend a hand!

-x-x-x-x-x-x-

Twin City

This little boys' room offers up a bevy of convenient storage options, from the double-door closet and overhead cabinets to the pullout drawers beneath each bed. But the custom book nooks made of reclaimed wood that form each kid's headboard are where the boys can really make the space their own. Besides books, they can also use the shelves to showcase trophies, toys, and other favorite trinkets.

In Plain Sight

It's tempting to shove toys and books in a closet or cabinet, shut the door, and forget the mess exists. But kids' stuff is so colorful and bright that it can make a fun display when stored out in the open, like on this freestanding baby-blue shelf. The open shelf also makes it easier for little ones to grab what they want and return it when they're done.

-x-x-x-x-x-x-

Cubby Club

This L-shaped storage unit outfitted with fabric bins was already organized, even without the easy-to-read labels. But once the labels were affixed to the removable bins, storage instantly became user-friendly. Now the kids know where each item is and where it should be returned. You can try this idea with vintage flash cards, too.

Time for Bed

-x-x-x-x-x-x-

Even the bed is tucked away in this everything-has-its-place kid's room in Georgia. In addition to the little table holding books and collections, a trio of baskets hidden under the bed provides extra storage, saves on floor space, and each is easy for kids to reach.

QUIET
IS REQUESTED FOR THE BENEFIT
OF THOSE WHO HAVE RETIRED

Practical Magic!

Use vintage trash cans to store board games and wooden blocks.

Taking Care of Business

Kids are busy these days, attending play dates, soccer games, homework sessions, and more. So they need a place to get their daily tasks done. A subdivided desk like this one can help. The different sections keep supplies tidy and leave room for other office necessities—like a retro rotary phone, of course!

-x-x-x-x-x-x-

Desk Job

Craft time became even more fun in this cute art nook. The piece of wood installed between two shelves forms a spacious workstation, and the metal pegboard on the wall is a wonderful display place for kids' nook-inspired artwork.

-x-x-x-x-x-x-

Toy Story

A retro toy and book collection feels right at home on this rusty reclaimed metal shelf. The throwback theme continues with the rack's organizational solutions. Instead of using bookends to keep the reading material in place, here, the homeowner opted for an old wooden box and vintage galvanized tin.

Outdoors

Outdoor spaces all too easily become dumping grounds for shovels, unused planters, and other gardening goods. Create defined areas you'll want to visit with these sunny ideas.

-x-x-x-x-x-x-

Garden Variety

Bright ideas were in full bloom in this lush garden space. The DIY potting table consists of an old door atop some galvanized containers, and a metal bucket hanging from the potting table contains handheld garden tools. In keeping with the reclaimed theme, a vintage Coke crate holds a cluster of flowers.

ROOM FOR IT ALL

This rustic shed houses a neatly arranged— and well-stocked!—kitchenette.

Cola Crate

An old wooden soda pop crate holds a medley of goods, including thermoses, flatware, and plastic straws.

Woven Basket

A shallow basket just barely fits between the top of the fridge and the bottom of the storage unit. (Seems like a good spot to hide your favorite treats from the rest of the family!)

Magnetic Board

Ideal for displaying family pics, postcards, and other little keepsakes.

Mason Jars

Decanted snacks fill the lidded jars, which look nice and orderly lined up on the shelves.

Stacking Shelves

This shelf setup works well for just about everything. Here, it contains snacks, mugs, and bowls—even some outdoor lanterns.

Patio Seating

The bar is open! This alfresco sitting area is all about multitasking.
Topping a barrel with a piece of glass makes an instant table and creates
covered storage for out-of-season outdoor cushions. And a fold-open
prep station is great for slicing fruit for drinks. The DIY cabinet also
conceals bar utensils after closing time.

Wonder Wall

All this garage needed to totally transform it was a trio of easily installed peg rails on one of the walls. Now garden tools live harmoniously next to rubber boots, sun hats, and woven totes. On the floor, metal trash cans with lids and customized labels hold mulch, compost, and topsoil.

MULCH

COMPOST

TOPSOIL

-x-x-x-x-x-x-

Divide and Conquer

When it comes to organization, old soda pop crates can be a gardener's best friend. The divided sections make it easy to contain a variety of items at once, from bulbs and plants to pots and tools. With their convenient handles, the durable crates are also super easy to move around.

-x-x-x-x-x-x-

Locker Room

Outdoor gear has a playful place to call home in this vibrant space. Old lockers act as storage for the whole family. Every guy and gal gets a locker, just like school days, so they can keep their stuff in one place.

Offices

Storage needs in an office often
exceed the size of your desk's
humble drawers. Expand your
horizons with charming cabinets and
outside-the-box organizers.

-x-x-x-x-x-x-x-

Safe Keeping

A corner of this Georgia office makes great use of a variety of yesteryear finds. From the old wooden cabinet that houses paperwork to the wall-mounted vintage chalkboard that acts as a note board, every piece has been given new life. But what really locks in the room's from-another-time theme is the antique safe used for extra storage.

ROOM FOR IT ALL

Teeming with unexpected storage ideas, this brightly painted craft station inspires creativity.

Wooden Spoons

The narrow handles of kitchen spoons are just the right size for holding spools of ribbon. Just wall-mount two brackets for each spoon to rest across.

Berry Baskets

These sturdy one-pint produce baskets aren't just for the farmers' market anymore. Here, hanging on the wall, they hold all kinds of crafty goodness.

Flower Frog

Business cards fit snugly in a vintage flower frog.

Old Dowels

These wooden rods are great for keeping gift wrap or kraft paper within easy reach. Plus, depending on the wrapping paper, the setup can make for a pattern-happy display.

Clean Jars

Small glass jars filled with buttons, string, and ribbons make the contents tidy, contained, and easily seen.

Swift's Brookfield
PASTEURIZED PROCESS CHEESE
5 LBS. NET

Mail Call

For an office desk with little or no drawer space, an old mail sorter is a storage option worth writing home about. The piece doesn't take up much room, and its divided sections keep small items neatly contained, leaving the work surface free of clutter. Plus, unlike a messy drawer, its contents are always on view and easily retrieved.

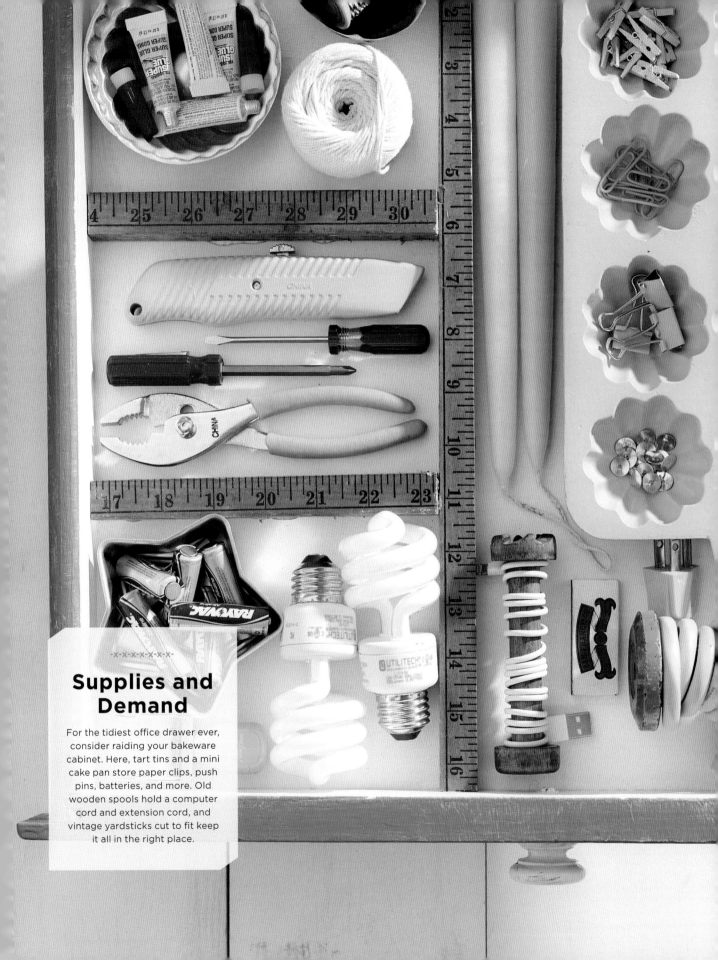

Supplies and Demand

For the tidiest office drawer ever, consider raiding your bakeware cabinet. Here, tart tins and a mini cake pan store paper clips, push pins, batteries, and more. Old wooden spools hold a computer cord and extension cord, and vintage yardsticks cut to fit keep it all in the right place.

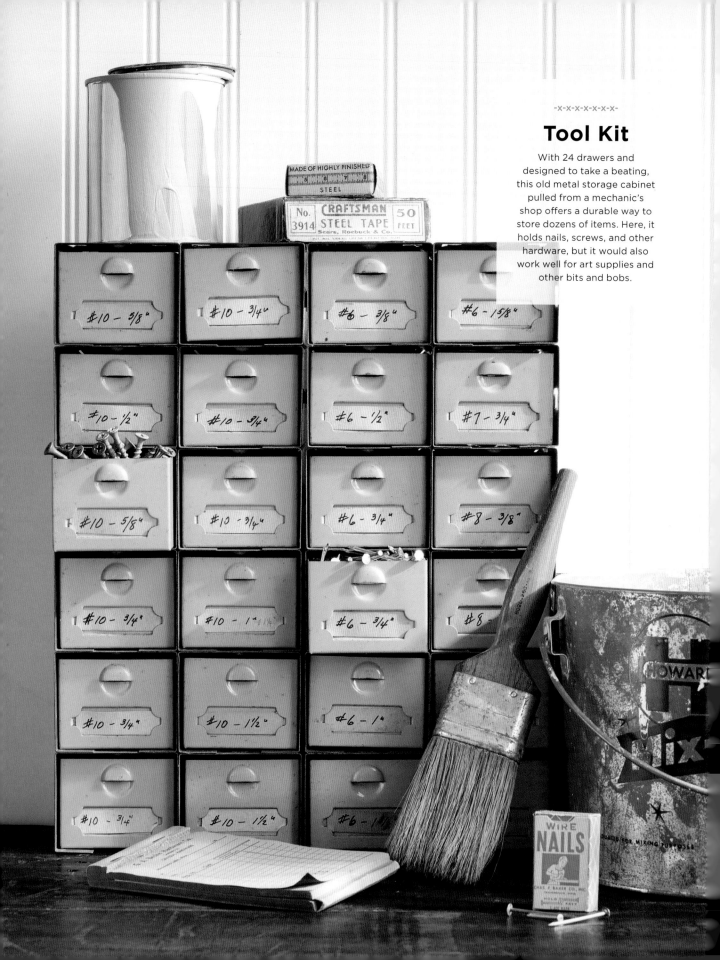

Tool Kit

With 24 drawers and designed to take a beating, this old metal storage cabinet pulled from a mechanic's shop offers a durable way to store dozens of items. Here, it holds nails, screws, and other hardware, but it would also work well for art supplies and other bits and bobs.

To-Dos

☐ Plan date night

☐ Call Mom

☐ Farmers' market

☑ Post Office

Practical Magic!

Install pegboard on the inside of closet doors, and hang a roll of kraft paper for a more memorable memo board.

-x-x-x-x-x-x-

Working It Out

If you don't have a dedicated office space in your home, it's possible to turn a closet into a work station. And with the right supplies, your new workroom could rival the stateliest of studies. Here, a corkboard wall is a place to pin notes and to-do lists, and three hardworking shelves hold books, files, and a desktop computer.

Organize Like an Expert

Introduction

You've made room for everything you love—and made it look good to boot. But organizing is not a "set it and forget it" situation. Now you have to maintain your collected, clutter-free home. You can't go back to your old house-in-disarray ways and expect to keep your home neat and tidy. We won't lie. This is going to take discipline. But you've worked so hard to accomplish your goals, it would be a shame to watch your success turn to shambles. That's why we have come up with "The Fab 15." Throughout the following pages, you'll find a detailed list of 15 tried-and-true steps to maintaining an organized home. We'll tell you what you need to do every single day to keep your place looking its best. We've also got weekly and monthly checklists you can follow to tackle chores, ranging from simple decluttering to hands-and-knees deep cleaning. In addition, we'll show you some pretty simple tricks that will make your life a whole lot easier, including how to best fold towels to make them fit in tight spaces, how to store certain finicky items properly, and where you can donate unused supplies that no longer fit in your newly organized life. We'll also tell you why you should embrace all-purpose pegboard and convert to decanting in your pantry. In short, we'll show you how to keep your home looking and feeling like a bona fide organizing guru lives there. Best of luck, and happy decanting! (We know you'll love it as much as we do.)

Tackle
"The Big Three"

Follow these three simple steps
every day, and you'll be guaranteed
to achieve a tidier, less cluttered
house—and a clearer mind, too!

Make the Bed

-x-x-x-x-x-x-

Besides making the room look neater and cleaner, research shows that making your bed every day has some beneficial psychological effects. According to one recent survey, 74 percent of people who reported making their bed every morning also reported that they felt accomplished at the end of the day. Folks who reported not making their bed? Only 50 percent felt accomplished. So if expending a few extra minutes each morning straightening the sheets means you can have a neat-as-a-pin sleep space and also feel proud of yourself when the day is done, we say grab those covers and get to tucking!

-x-x-x-x-x-x-

-x-x-x-x-x-x-

Skirt the Issue

Not only can a bed skirt hide an unsightly box spring, but it can also create hidden storage beneath the bed. To be sure you purchase a skirt that barely grazes the floor—like the one in this fetching bedroom in England—you'll need to get your bed's measurements: width, length, and drop (the length from the top of the foundation to the floor).

2

Clean As You Cook

-x-x-x-x-x-x-

This rule is in effect in most professional kitchens for one important reason: It prevents messes from becoming unmanageable. The last thing you want to do is spend hours preparing a meal for you and your family and then spend hours afterward cleaning it up. Plus, from a food-safety standpoint, cleaning as you go just makes good sense. To help keep your workspace spic and span while you cook, there are a few simple steps you can take.

-x-x-x-x-x-x-

Keep a damp kitchen towel in a convenient spot where you can grab it quickly to wipe up spills immediately.

-x-x-x-x-x-x-

Set up a garbage bowl on the counter where you can easily toss peels and scraps—it will reduce mess and save you trips to the garbage can or compost bin.

-x-x-x-x-x-x-

Soak pots and pans as soon as possible to cut down on scrubbing time.

-x-x-x-x-x-x-

-x-x-x-x-x-x-

Pretty in Pastel

When making dinner for friends
or family, the owners of this
bright and happy kitchen can fill
the apron-front sink with warm
soapy water to soak dishes and
pots. And their shelves are set up
for more efficient cooking and
serving: Everyday dishes sit on
lower levels for frequent retrieval,
and lesser-used items, like platters
and cake stands, live higher up.

-x-x-x-x-x-x-

All Sorted Out

The compartmentalized desktop shelf in this office nook is a dream for organization. The different-size sections can hold both decor and office supplies, and other slots can be left open for when it's time to sort the mail. The bin next to the desk makes for easy disposal of unwanted correspondence or promo mailers.

3

Sort
the Mail

-x-x-x-x-x-x-

With the massive amount
of junk mail that hits
mailboxes on a daily basis,
it's easy to feel buried in
real estate promotions,
supermarket ads, and other
fliers by the end of the week.
To avoid piles of papers—
and possibly misplacing
important post lost in the
madness—go through your
mail every day. Throw out
the unwanted promotional
pieces immediately. Then
open the letters and bills and
determine what's important.
Don't want or need it? In the
bin it goes—stat. Important
pieces should be put in a
place where you won't forget
about them. If you don't have
a desk with shelves, you can
buy a standard wall-mounted
mail holder online (or create
your own with wire baskets)
or opt for a desktop version
(again, baskets—wire
or otherwise—work great
for this).

-x-x-x-x-x-x-

Create a Weekly Cleaning and Decluttering Routine

For every day of the week, choose a room in your home to tidy up, and you won't wind up with a house in disarray come Sunday night. You can follow this handy checklist or come up with your own. If you don't want to tackle the kitchen on Monday, for example, then do it on Thursday, and hit the home office on Monday instead. Whatever works for your schedule is best. Just don't skip a day!

Entryway

-x-x-x-x-x-x-

☐ Check the space, and pick up any items that need to be put back in place.

☐ Straighten the benches, shelves, cubbies, or bins.

☐ Clean the mirrors.

☐ Vacuum the stairs and landings.

☐ Vacuum or mop the floor.

Practical Magic!

The owner of this Wisconsin mudroom created a three-zone entryway: An out-of-reach upper shelf holds items that aren't used on a regular basis. In the middle, wall hooks are a catchall spot for daily-worn jackets, hats, and leashes. And a bottom shelf acts as a bench, good when you need to slip shoes on or off.

MONDAY

Kitchen

-x-x-x-x-x-x-

☐ Clear off countertops, table, and island, putting everything back in its place (including small appliances), then clean.

☐ Clean the sink.

☐ Discard food and beverages that have expired dates.

☐ Straighten pantry shelves and cabinets.

☐ Wipe the inside and outside of trash and recycling bins.

☐ Sweep and mop the floor.

Practical Magic!

The display of well-worn wood cutting boards in this bright white kitchen adds warmth and frees up drawer space for less counter-worthy items.

To Do
- sew buttons
- pick up dry cleaning
- wash sheets

Bathrooms & Laundry Room

-x-x-x-x-x-x-

- ☐ Clear off countertops in both spaces, putting everything back in its place, then clean.

- ☐ Empty the trash bins in both spaces, then clean them inside and out.

- ☐ Change and launder the bath mats and towels.

- ☐ Clean the mirrors.

- ☐ Clean the toilets, bathtubs, showers, and sinks.

- ☐ Sweep and mop the floor.

Practical Magic!

The salvaged ladder suspended from the ceiling in this sunny laundry room holds woven baskets for extra linen storage.

WEDNESDAY

Bedrooms & Closet

-x-x-x-x-x-x-

☐ Clear off the side tables,
putting books back
on the shelf, papers in the
recycling bin, and water
glasses in the kitchen.

☐ Change and launder the
sheets and pillowcases.

☐ Straighten the dresser.

☐ Empty the trash bins.

☐ Put clean clothes
in the closet
and dirty clothes
in the hamper.

☐ Straighten the clothes
and shoes inside closet.

☐ Vacuum or sweep
the floor.

Practical Magic!

Always squeeze in bedside
storage, even if you have to
get creative. In this calming
retreat, an antique chair
offers extra space for books
and a charming display for
some framed art.

Office

-x-x-x-x-x-x-

☐ Empty the trash
and recycling bins.

☐ Shred any papers
deemed unimportant.

☐ Attend to mail
that needs a response.

☐ Vacuum or sweep
the floor.

Practical Magic!

No desk drawers? No problem! Tuck a stylish free-standing container, like the simple white pail in this cheerful office, underneath your work station for a little extra storage.

FRIDAY

Living Room

-x-x-x-x-x-

- ☐ Pick up and return items to their appointed places (books, blankets, toys, remotes).

- ☐ Straighten the coffee table and side tables.

- ☐ Rotate the sofa cushions.

- ☐ Vacuum the upholstery.

- ☐ Vacuum or sweep the floor.

Practical Magic!

Keeping shelf contents to complementary hues—like the pottery pieces in this New Jersey home—creates a calm scene, even when the shelves are packed full.

Outdoors

-x-x-x-x-x-x-

☐ Survey the living areas, like patios, decks, and porches, pick up out-of-place items, and put them where they belong (outdoor kid toys, pet toys, grilling equipment).

☐ Rotate the outdoor-furniture cushions.

☐ Sweep the floor.

☐ Tidy up the garage and any outbuildings, such as potting sheds.

Practical Magic!

This well-organized potting shed is wall to wall with fresh storage ideas, including a pegboard for gardening tools, wooden crates for keeping extra supplies, and wall hooks holding a variety of sun hats for when it's time to hit the garden.

ORGANIZE LIKE AN EXPERT **177**

NO. **3**

Create a Monthly Deep-Cleaning Routine

Unlike the weekly routine, this to-do list tackles household chores that go beyond simple decluttering and surface cleaning. These duties are more intensive (that gnarly oven is going to require some elbow grease), so you're only going to tackle them once a month. As with the weekly list, this routine can be tweaked to fit your household's lifestyle. If your family is more into ordering takeout than trying new recipes, for example, then maybe that oven isn't so gnarly after all, and might not need a cleaning each month.

BATHROOMS

Scrub the grout.

Wipe inside the medicine cabinets.

Wipe down the tub and shower surrounds.

Clean the bathroom scales.

Flush the drains with vinegar, boiling water, and baking soda.

BEDROOMS

Wash duvet covers, pillow protectors, mattress pads, and shams.

Clean under the beds.

KITCHEN

Wipe down the vent hood.

Wipe down the cabinet doors.

Clean the oven inside and out.

Clean the refrigerator and freezer inside and out.

Clean the microwave inside and out.

Flush the drains with vinegar, boiling water, and baking soda.

LAUNDRY ROOM

Wipe the washer and dryer inside and out.

Wipe down the cabinet doors and countertops.

Wipe the trash and recycling bins inside and outside.

THROUGHOUT

Wipe interior and exterior doors and trim.

Wipe the switch plates.

Clean the windows.

Dust the ceilings, shutters, furniture, shelves, and baseboards.

Dust the ceiling fans.

Clean the light fixtures.

Dust air vents.

Vacuum inside the furniture.

Vacuum window treatments, moldings, and windowsills.

NO. 4

Create a Hardworking Drop Zone

Everyday items, like backpacks and bills, can wreak havoc on even the most curated, collected home. Avoid the pitfall by designating a home command station, a placefor all family members to deposit their stuff. Because every home and family are different, you'll have to carve out a space that fits your floor plan and lifestyle. While entryways and mudrooms are typical drop-zone locales, in your home it could be the kitchen, an office nook, or a back hallway. Depending on the room you have, you could add wall hooks, shelves, or labeled cubbies to handle everyone's belongings. This is also the space where you can keep track of social schedules and household tasks with an oversize calendar, chalkboard, or dry-erase board.

-x-x-x-x-x-x-

Chalk It Up

Here, a DIY chalkboard wall calendar ensures no one misses an important date, including vet visits, mortgage payments, and no-school days. If making your own, be sure to buy enough chalkboard paint to apply at least two coats. The more coats, the smoother the surface will be.

Fold Your Linens Just So

When it comes to folding bath towels, hand towels, or any other kinds of towels, there's one method many experts suggest for keeping them looking neat and fitting as many pieces into one place as possible. It's called the trifold system, and just like the name implies, it's a quick, three-step process:

-x-x x-x-	-x-x x-x-	-x-x **3** x-x-
Lay the towel flat, back side facing up.	Fold the towel in thirds—bring one long edge just beyond the center of the towel, then fold the other edge in, overlapping the other side by about an inch.	Fold the towel in half.

Beachy Keen

The bathroom in this 1940s Hamptons beach house is small and storage is open for all to see, so it's important that towels be folded as neatly as possible. Here, an old wooden bench— one of the homeowners' many tag-sale treasures—serves as under-sink storage. Two-tiered pieces like this one are great for separating linens into shorter, more manageable stacks.

NO. 6

Treat Labels
Like Artwork

Labels help implement a system and put the whole household on the same page. Plus, they elevate the look of a space. Use them in kitchens, pantries, kids spaces, mudrooms, and more. And get creative with them! Any type of label can help get your space organized, but the only type that can reflect your unique personality lies inside your own head.

-x-x-x-x-x-x-

Coat the lids of mason jars with chalkboard paint and write in the name of each jar's contents—this is good for any item you can store in a drawer, where only the jar tops can be seen.

-x-x-x-x-x-x-

Affix vintage flash cards to kids' toy bins so they know what's inside.

-x-x-x-x-x-x-

Use plain paper tags and alphabet stamps to create custom labels for pantry bins.

-x-x-x-x-x-x-

Same, Same

Uniformity is the key to the orderliness of this kitchen's open-shelving system. Decanted dry goods in similar glass jars are identified by chalkboard labels, each neatly placed along the bottom edge of the jars.

NO. **7**

Make It
Picture Perfect

———

Once you have your clutter curated, take a picture you can refer to later showing what goes where. This system is especially helpful for "living gallery" walls where you regularly use the contents—say, hats, aprons, or baskets. And snap pics of closet interiors and china cabinets, too. Once something gets out of place, it's not always easy to remember exactly where it came from, but if you keep photo albums of each area in your smartphone, you can quickly refresh your memory.

-x-x-x-x-x-x-

Woven Together

A collection of woven bags and baskets brings form and function to this light
and airy mudroom/laundry room. A spacious tray hung vertically adds warmth
to the space as well as a ledge for stashing odds and ends. Roomy totes offer
a stylish way to store everything from socks waiting for their match to tools
ready for a day out in the garden.

Embrace Pegboard

Hardware stores, pharmacies, and other retail outlets have been using pegboard for ages to display their goods across their sales floors and at their counters. There's good reason for this: The system keeps items neatly on display, it's easily rearranged, and the material is super durable. So it's no surprise that pegboard is also the ultimate workhorse for affordable home organization. Use it in craft rooms to hold wrapping paper and spools of ribbon. Install it in garages for keeping tools at hand. Or try it in your utility room to store scrub brushes, brooms, lint rollers, and more. It works in almost every room of the house. One common complaint about pegboard, however, is that traditional hooks can fall out easily when an item is removed. To keep this from happening, you can glue the hooks in place with a hot-glue gun.

Board Members

Here, a collection of hand mixers fills a pegboard wall in the kitchen. This ultimate storage solution is convenient for all sorts of kitchen supplies. Even legendary chef Julia Child famously had a wall-size pegboard in her home kitchen to store her pots and pans.

NO. 9

Pay Attention to Expiration Dates

While we love patina, there's no need to accrue a collection of expired items like foods, cosmetics, art paints, and more. Set up a regular system of checking and tossing expired items and you'll be sure to maintain a tidy space. Once a week, go through the fridge and check labels, throwing away what's no longer good. Assess your cosmetics every few months. Mascara, for example, expires in 90 days, if used daily. The typical lifespan of art supplies, like paint and liquid glue, is anywhere from one to two years, so make a plan to clean out the craft closet at least once a year.

-x-x-x-x-x-x-

Toiletry Case

This three-tiered caddy is a handy way to contain daily-use bathroom necessities like toothpaste, hairspray, and toner. For toiletries like these, if a product has a shelf life of six months, the clock starts when you first use it, not when you purchase it.

NO. 10

When In Doubt, Let Color Guide You

———

While there are some items in the home that won't benefit from being organized by color (kitchen goods like pots, serving platters, and baking dishes are much better grouped by size and shape, for example), plenty of other pieces could really use the rainbow treatment. Clothes, of course, are great candidates for this method, as grouping them by color will aid in outfit selection on those hectic, late-for-work mornings. But also try color coding art supplies and linens. Not only will it help you easily grab what you need when you need it, but it will also gives you a treat to look at. Arranging books by color works, too, even if literary purists don't agree. A color-coded bookshelf is much easier to keep organized—as opposed to grouping by author, alphabetically by title, or genre— especially in children's rooms where you want them to pick up after themselves.

-x-x-x-x-x-x-

True Colors

In this darling girl's room, an angled built-in holds vintage books sorted by color. Not only does this arrangement delight the eye, it also helps the books' owner keep her shelves organized. When it's time to put a book back after reading, she can easily tell where it belongs.

-x-x-x-x-x-x-

Rainbow Connection

The long, flowing ribbons in this well-organized craft room are grouped by color
(hello, ROYGBIV!), making it easy to tell where they should be returned to on the wall. An old
yardstick with a series of hooks acts as a DIY rack for the ribbons, which hang from simple
wooden loops. This setup keeps ribbons from knotting, and the rainbow effect is a visual delight.

All That Glitters

Spice racks installed on the inside of a craft room door are a nifty way to hold glass jars filled with glitter. And the color-based organizing system shows off the subtle differences between the glitters' various hues—important when a project calls for the just-right shade of sparkle.

Keep It Where You Use It

If you store items near where they're needed, you'll create a more efficient space and save time on regular tasks. Though this rule applies to the entire house, one great example is bathroom cleaning supplies. Storing them upstairs near the actual bathrooms, not just in the laundry room with other cleaning supplies, will make your life a lot easier. And the same goes for laundry-room essentials. If you occasionally mend clothes in the laundry, tuck your needle and thread there. Don't store them in a bathroom drawer and hope you can remember where they are when you happen to run across a missing button.

-x-x-x-x-x-x-

Purple Reign

Washing clothes doesn't feel like a chore in this bright laundry room, especially since all laundry-day essentials are right where they need to be. From the bottle of bleach on top of the washing machine to the jars of clothespins and multicolored thread perched on open shelves, all necessary items are easy to find.

NO. 12

Decant It

———

The packaging on many products we buy at the store can be, well, ugly, to put it bluntly. But that's not the only reason we're big fans of decanting whenever possible. Besides giving a more artful look to a space, decanting has several other upsides. In the pantry, for example, transferring dry goods like flour and sugar to clear containers lets you see when your supply is running low. Using airtight containers also means food is fresher longer. And, most important for organizing purposes, decanted items take up less space than bulky boxes and bags of varying sizes. We also love decanting soaps and detergents in the laundry room for the same reasons.

-x-x-x-x-x-x-

Kitchen Confidential

In this Colorado farmhouse kitchen, the homeowners decanted their dry goods into glass jars.
This method reduces visual clutter and makes it easy to keep track of the quantities on hand. The
pantry is organized in a helpful zone approach: baskets of snacks on the lower level, decanted dry
goods on the middle shelves, and overstock items in baskets overhead.

Store It Correctly

To keep them in tiptop shape, some items require special storage climates and conditions. Wine is notoriously tricky, for example. And paint also has a few special requirements. To keep it from drying out, paint must be stored in a cool, dry place away from direct sunlight and in a spot with the temperature above freezing. Silver pieces and flatware need special attention, too. To help prevent tarnishing, they should be stored in an area without high heat or high humidity—a china cabinet in your dining room, for example, instead of an attic or basement.

-x-x-x-x-x-x-

China Doll

The drawer of a china cabinet—like this antique piece filled with Mottahedeh china—is a great place to store silverware. To slow down the tarnishing process, line the drawer with flannel cloth. You can also buy flannel bags to protect larger items like teapots, trays, and bowls.

NO. **14**

Done With It?
Donate It!

You probably already know of some places in your town that need regular donations of gently used clothing. But have you considered donating items such as unused craft supplies? A good organizing method means you shouldn't have to part with anything. But after revamping your craft station or studio you may find you have an abundance of a certain supply, or maybe you have materials left over from a crafting project that just didn't pan out. If so, check with your local community centers, schools, and shelters. They just might be in need of some of the things you want to get rid of. There are also several nonprofit groups across the country specifically seeking donated craft supplies.

-x-x x-x-

Based in New York, Materials for the Arts accepts a wide variety of supplies, including fabric, paper, beads, and paint. They then distribute the supplies to public schools and nonprofit organizations.

-x-x x-x-

Donations to The Dreaming Zebra Foundation in Oregon help the nonprofit provide art and music supplies to underprivileged kids around the world.

-x-x x-x-

A nonprofit crafts collective for refugee women, Colorado-based A Little Something accepts donated supplies for use in the women's handmade crafts, which they sell at local fairs and festivals.

-x-x-x-x-x-x-

In Living Color

This rainbow-colored array of washi tape looks great displayed on an old store rack. Consider a similar setup for your own craft supplies. Then, when you've got everything arranged just so, assess what you have left over and look for a nonprofit organization that accepts donations of unused supplies. You'll keep the items out of the landfill and help a needy group in the process.

NO. **15**

Keep Like
Items Together

———

From an organizational standpoint, no matter what
the item is, the place it best belongs is where all its
mates are. You have a sock drawer, right? And maybe
even a jewelry cabinet? And possibly a games closet?
When you need a pair of socks or earrings or a board
game, you want to go looking for them in one spot
and one spot only. Well, the same concept applies
to your collections. If you have multiples of one type
of item—say, flower vases or vintage linens or brass
candleholders—keeping them all in one place makes
for easy retrieval. And depending on how you arrange
them, they could make a beautiful display, too.

-x-x-x-x-x-x-

Material World

This antique armoire in a 1920s California cottage houses hundreds of vintage grain sacks and French linens from the homeowner's vast collection. By keeping all the linens together in one place, rather than in multiple closets or cabinets, she always knows where to look when she wants to grab a particular piece. Use this method for just about any collection you have.

Credits

⸻

Thank you for purchasing
Get Organized, Keep Everything

-x-x-x-x-x-

Visit our online store to find more great products
from *Country Living* and save 20% off your next purchase.

HEARST